The Berenstain Bears®
GET A CHECKUP

Stan & Jan Berenstain

Reader's Digest **Kids**

Westport, Connecticut

Mama, may we
go out and play?

No. We are going
to the doctor today.

But we're not sick!
We are well!

It does no good
to stomp and yell.
This checkup card
that came by mail
says, *Be here at two.
Come without fail.*

Phooey on checkups!
They're such a bore!
Why do we need them?
What are they for?

Checkups are how
the doctor can tell
that you and your sister
are both staying well.

So come along, dears.
And please do not fuss.
You know that your
health is important to us.

Do you think Doctor Grizzly
will give us a shot?

I can't say whether
she will or not.
But it may be time
for your booster shot.

BOOSTER SHOT?

Stop the car!

We're on the wrong road!

Stuff and nonsense.

It's not the wrong road.

Turn back! You ran over

a great big toad!

Nonsense and stuff.

There was no toad.

What a crowd!

Let's not stay!

We'll be waiting

here all day!

DR. GRIZZLY
IS
IN

Waiting here
will help us learn
to calmly and quietly
wait for our turn.

Brother and Sister!
Well, hello there!
Take off everything
except your underwear!

Now, one at a time,
hop up on this table!
I'll give you a hand
if you are not able.

Now, just pull up
your undershirts.

And please let me know
if anything hurts.

Well, my dears,
what do you say?

No problem, Doctor!
I feel okay!

Do you know what this is?

I don't think so.

Nope.

This is called
a stethoscope.
It lets me listen
to your heart.
Then I write *fine*
on your chart.

Doctor Grizzly,
before you start,
I'd like to know why
you need that chart.

I can't keep everything
in my head.
That's why I keep
this chart instead.

So every time
you cubs show up,
I can check your chart
as you grow up.

Now, for your ears.

I hope they're clean.

As clean a pair
as I have seen!
Next I'll whisper
in your ear.
Listen and tell me
what you hear.

You said, "So far,
your checkups are good!"

Hear that, Mama?
Let's knock on wood!

Now, your eyes.
Read the smallest letters
you can see.

A, P, R, I, O, U, Z.

Your turn, Brother.

A, P, R, I, O, U, Z.

Now, step on the scale.

We'll see what you weigh.

All right, Doctor.

What does it say?

Thirty-seven for you.
Forty-six for Brother.

I'm proud of you both.
And you should be proud
of each other!

Yessiree!
Those cubs are healthy,
just like me!
I knew they would pass
that checkup test.
Er . . . may I get weighed?

Yes, of course. Be my guest!

Well now, Papa,
how about you?
You weigh two hundred
and fifty-two!

That wasn't bad.
It was almost fun.
Well, so long, Doc.
I guess we're done.

We have done
quite a lot.
But there's one more thing
I almost forgot.
It's time to get
your booster shot.

Doc, are we healthy
or are we not?
Why do we need
a booster shot?

This shot has special
medicine in it.
Yes, it may hurt
for half a minute.

But it can keep you well
year after year!
What do you say
to that, my dear?

I say, *"Ouch,"*
but it wasn't so bad.

Are you as brave
as your sister, my lad?

One last thing—
Where is my prescription pad?

For us?

No. This is something
for your dad.

Two hundred fifty-two
is very, very, very bad!

But, Doc, I'll starve!
I'll waste away!

See you in six months.
Have a nice day!

Carrot sticks? I have
an extra one or two.

No thanks, Dad. The carrot sticks
are just for you!